American

JAZZ

COUNT
BASIE

JOANNE MATTERN

Mitchell Lane
PUBLISHERS
P.O. Box 196
Hockessin, Delaware 19707

American JAZZ

Benny Goodman

Bessie Smith

Billie Holiday

Charlie Parker

Count Basie

Dizzy Gillespie

Louis Armstrong

Miles Davis

Ornette Coleman

Scott Joplin

Copyright © 2013 by Mitchell Lane Publishers

PUBLISHER'S NOTE: The facts on which this book is based have been thoroughly researched. Documentation of such research can be found on page 44. While every possible effort has been made to ensure accuracy, the publisher will not assume liability for damages caused by inaccuracies in the data, and makes no warranty on the accuracy of the information contained herein.

Printing   1   2   3   4   5   6   7   8   9

Library of Congress
Cataloging-in-Publication Data

Mattern, Joanne, 1963–
  Count Basie / by Joanne Mattern.
    p. cm. — (American jazz)
  Includes bibliographical references and index.
  ISBN 978-1-61228-270-1 (library bound)
  1. Basie, Count, 1904-1984--Juvenile literature.
  2. Jazz musicians—United States—Biography—
Juvenile literature. 3. African American
musicians—Biography—Juvenile literature. I.
Title.
  ML3930.B33M38 2012
  781.65092—dc23
  [B]
                                    2012008629
eBook ISBN: 9781612283463

                                    PLB

Contents

Chapter 1

The Man at the Piano

John Hammond could not believe his ears. It was a cold November night in 1935, and the young music critic had just left a performance by his friend, big band leader Benny Goodman, at Chicago's Congress Hotel. After the show, Hammond got into his car to drive back to his room. As always, he switched on the big shortwave radio in the front seat. This was no ordinary radio. Hammond spent a lot of time on the road, driving from his home in New York City to listen to jazz musicians around the country, and he liked to keep up with the latest music. His shortwave radio made it possible to listen to bands playing far out of the range of a normal radio.

That night, Hammond's radio picked up a jazz band playing in Kansas City, Missouri. Hammond had heard a lot of jazz in his time, but never anything like this. The band didn't have a lot of instruments compared to other big bands of the day, and each player was something special. Hammond listened as different band members took solos, amazed by how well the band played together while still featuring each artist. Most exciting of all was the band's rhythm section, made up of bass, drums, and piano. The rhythm section provided a strong, steady beat, yet the music was smooth and elegant.

Hammond had to know who this band was. Finally, the song ended and the announcer came on the air. The announcer said that listeners had just heard Count Basie and His Barons of Rhythm, playing live at the

Reno Club in Kansas City. Hammond was surprised. He had seen Count Basie before, playing piano in a club in New York City, but he didn't know Basie was now leading a band of his own. He wanted to hear more—and he thought other Americans would also want to. As he drove into the night, he started to plan.

At the time he was playing at the Reno, Count Basie's band was smaller than most bands of that era. It was common for "big bands" to have twelve to sixteen members. Basie's band had only eight. Basie led the band and played the piano. The band also included bassist Walter Page; drummer Jo Jones; four horn players, including trumpets and saxophones; and a vocalist named Jimmy Rushing, who performed on some of the band's songs. Later, when Basie began performing in larger concert halls in New York and other cities, he had to add members, especially in the horn section, to produce the big, rich sound that big band audiences were used to.

Back in Kansas City, Count Basie was hearing about John Hammond as well. At that time, Hammond was writing articles for a jazz magazine called *DownBeat*. He began mentioning Basie in his articles, explaining how he had heard Basie's band on the radio and thought they were fantastic. He also mentioned that he would like Basie to write to him. Basie was flattered, but he wasn't sure what to think about Hammond's comments, and he made no effort to contact him.

After Hammond had mentioned Basie a few more times, the bandleader finally sat down and wrote him a letter. Hammond wrote back right away and said he was coming to Kansas City to hear the Basie band. Basie didn't believe that anyone would come all the way from New York to Kansas City just to hear a band, so he put Hammond's letter out of his mind.

Hammond wasn't kidding. As Basie recalled in his autobiography, "It was a Sunday night and we were on the air, and this very young cat just came right on up there and sat on the bench beside me. I didn't pay much attention to him at first, because actually that was something that used to happen very often, especially at the Reno. . . . I looked around,

John Hammond leans over Count Basie's shoulder. Hammond discovered and guided the careers of many jazz artists, as well as folk and rock artists during the 1960s, 1970s, and early 1980s.

and that's when I saw that the young fellow sitting there was a complete stranger to me."[1]

Hammond introduced himself and stayed to talk to Basie after the show. The two men got along instantly, despite their different backgrounds. As Basie put it, "He liked what I liked. He liked the blues."[2]

Meeting John Hammond changed Count Basie's career forever. Hammond went back to New York City and began talking about Basie and his band to everyone he met. Even though Hammond was only in his mid-twenties, he knew a lot of musicians and people in the recording industry and was well respected in the jazz world. Through Hammond, Basie was offered a recording contract with Decca Records and later an even better contract with Brunswick Records. Hammond also brought

Count Basie joins author Richard Wright at a recording session in 1940. The sharply dressed men are wearing suits that were the height of fashion at that time.

Basie to the attention of promoters who booked concerts and tours. Before long, Basie and his band would leave Kansas City to tour Chicago and New York. They would become one of the best-known and most influential bands of the swing era.

John Hammond

John Hammond has been called the most important non-musician in the history of jazz. Born to a wealthy family in New York City in 1910, he became interested in music at a young age. He especially loved jazz and often traveled to Harlem to hear musicians and attend shows at the clubs there. Although he was white and most of the musicians in Harlem were black, Hammond connected with them because of his love of music. He later became one of the strongest voices in favor of integration in the music industry. Legendary folk singer Pete Seeger said, "Jazz became integrated ten years before baseball largely because of John Hammond."[3]

Through his work as a music critic and writer as well as a producer, Hammond brought many jazz artists to the attention of both record companies and audiences. He was a major force behind Benny Goodman, who was known as the King of Swing (and who later married Hammond's sister); and he also promoted singer Billie Holiday. He continued to be influential after folk and rock became the most popular forms of music during the 1960s and 1970s. He is credited with promoting Bob Dylan and Bruce Springsteen and signing both singers to Columbia Records. He also signed legendary blues guitarist Stevie Ray Vaughan. Hammond was inducted into the Rock and Roll Hall of Fame in 1986. He died in 1987.

The Boy from Red Bank

William Basie was born on August 21, 1904, in the small town of Red Bank, New Jersey. Called Bill as a child, he was the second son of Harvey Lee and Lilly Ann Childs Basie. His older brother, Leroy, died when Bill was very young, so Bill was raised as an only child.

Harvey and Lilly Ann originally came from Virginia but moved to New Jersey after they got married. Harvey worked on several large estates owned by rich white families in the Red Bank area. For a while, he worked as a coachman for a man named Judge White, caring for the horses that were used to pull carriages in those days before cars were common. Basie had fond memories of the judge's beautiful estate on the banks of the Shrewsbury River. He enjoyed going to work with his father when he was old enough to help with the horses. After Judge White replaced his horses with cars, Harvey Basie worked for the judge as a groundskeeper, tending the gardens of the estate. He did the same for other families in the area.

Lilly Ann also worked for rich families. She did laundry at home, washing and ironing clothes by hand and then delivering the clean clothes back to their owners. Bill often helped his mother with the laundry. He carried the heavy baskets of wet clothes outside to dry on clotheslines. During the winter, he cleared ice off the clotheslines and helped his mother fold and then deliver the clean laundry around town on his sled.

The Basies did not make much money for all their hard work. Harvey earned about forty dollars a month and Lilly Ann made about fifty cents for each load of laundry. Still, they were able to save enough money to buy a small house in Red Bank, where Bill was raised. Bill often felt bad about how hard his parents had to work to provide for the family. He recalled in his autobiography, "I used to look at all those big baskets of clothes, and as far as I was concerned, that was too much work for the little change she was getting paid."[1] Bill vowed that in the future he would make life better for his parents. He once drew a picture of a car and gave it to his mother with the promise that someday he would make enough money to buy her a real one.

Bill's other big desire was to become a musician. His mother knew how to play the piano, and she was Bill's first music teacher. Bill also worked piano exercises with Judge White's daughter. Later, the Basies hired a German woman, Miss Vandevere, to teach Bill for twenty-five cents a lesson. Bill enjoyed the piano, but his favorite instrument was the drums. His father bought him an inexpensive drum kit, and Bill practiced hard. In time, he became good enough to perform in public.

However, Bill heard other drummers and realized they were much better than he was. He gave up his dream of becoming a professional drummer and went back to the piano. It soon became clear that he had real musical talent and could play just about any song he heard. He also learned the basics of reading music, although he confessed that he never was very good at it. Because he could hear a song and then play pretty much anything he heard, Bill did not pay much attention to learning all the rules. He just played.

Bill did not spend all his time at the piano. There were plenty of ways for a young boy to have fun in Red Bank. Some of his favorite times occurred when traveling circuses or carnivals came to town and set up on a vacant lot near his house. Bill often helped these traveling shows set up and then attended the shows. These events gave him an early taste of show business and a strong desire to be a traveling entertainer.

Bill also enjoyed going to the movies. In those days, movies were silent and most theaters had a piano player who played music to go along with the film. Bill spent many hours at a Red Bank theater called the Palace. He often worked there in exchange for watching the movies for free. One day, the Palace's piano player called in sick and Bill volunteered to fill in. He did so well, he was invited back to play at the next showing.

Bill was soon playing in public more frequently. He and some of his friends performed in a vaudeville act at the Palace Theater. They also played at private parties in town, as well as at dances and clubs. Bill was not a teenager yet and was much too young to legally be allowed inside some of the clubs where he played. To get around this, he would sneak in by offering to help the musicians carry their instruments. Once he was inside and got a chance to play, no one complained about his age.

There was one big drawback to Bill's love of music: He was far more interested in music than he was in school. He missed so much school that he was left back many times. He didn't graduate from junior high until he was nineteen years old. Bill saw no point in going to high school. Instead, he decided his life would be devoted to playing music. When he was older, Bill said that quitting school was the

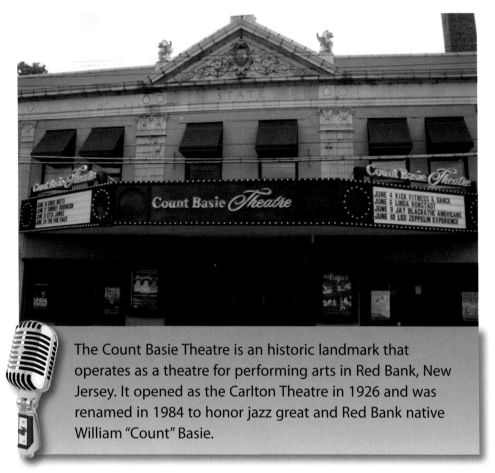

The Count Basie Theatre is an historic landmark that operates as a theatre for performing arts in Red Bank, New Jersey. It opened as the Carlton Theatre in 1926 and was renamed in 1984 to honor jazz great and Red Bank native William "Count" Basie.

worst decision he ever made. But at the time, it seemed like the right thing to do.

Bill spent the next few years playing in Red Bank and other nearby towns. During the summers, he teamed up with a friend named Elmer Williams, who played the saxophone, and the two traveled to the resort town of Asbury Park, New Jersey. Although they found work as musicians in a few different restaurants, Bill sometimes ended up parking cars to earn money. Still, he was determined to succeed and had no intention of returning to Red Bank. "We were musicians and we didn't ever think about making a living doing anything except playing," he later recalled.[2] Bill would soon get his chance, but he would have to leave New Jersey to find it.

Music in Silent Movies

The first movie was shown around 1895, but it wasn't until 1927 that "talkies," or movies with sound, became common. Until then, silent films were extremely popular. While the actors and actresses conveyed emotion through visual cues and exaggerated facial expressions and gestures, dialogue was printed on cards that were shown as part of the film. The only thing missing was music. To add music to the movie experience, showings of silent films almost always featured live music. Theaters in small towns usually had a pianist who played along with the movie, using the music to add to the atmosphere of the story and give the audience cues about what might happen next. Sad music might indicate heartbreak, for example, while fast, exciting music might accompany a chase scene. Theaters in big cities had more elaborate music, often provided by organists who could create many more sounds on the organ than on a piano. Organs could also contribute sound effects such as thunder or galloping horses. Some city theaters even had small bands.

While most movies came with sheet music to play, musicians often improvised. They also had cue sheets that told them what scenes to look out for and what type of music would be appropriate. During the height of the silent-movie era, movies provided the largest source of employment for musicians in America. When movies with sound were introduced, this part of the music industry was eliminated.

Ben Turpin (left) and Charlie Chaplin in *His New Job*. Chaplin was one of the most creative and influential personalities of the silent-film era.

From New York to Kansas City

In 1924, Bill Basie was ready for something new. He had not made much of a success as a musician in Asbury Park, but he had made a lot of new friends and contacts. One of those new friends was originally from Harlem, a section of uptown Manhattan in New York City that had the largest African American population in the United States. This man told Basie all about the thriving music scene in Harlem and encouraged Basie and his friend Elmer Williams to go there. He even offered the young men a place to stay at his apartment. Basie and Williams jumped at the chance, and at the end of the summer season, they took the train north from Asbury Park to Harlem.

From the start, Basie loved Harlem. The streets were full of music, and it didn't take long for him to start showing off his talents. After hearing music coming from a club one night, he met a bandleader named Lou Henry and asked him if he could play with them. When Henry said yes, Basie was quick to show off. "I went into my little act," he later wrote, "making fancy runs and throwing my hands all up in the air and flashing my fingers."[1] The audience liked Basie, and so did Henry. He quickly offered both Basie and Williams a job touring with his vaudeville act, Katie Krippen and Her Kiddies.

After a few weeks of rehearsal in Harlem, Basie was on the road. Katie Krippen was the stage name of Henry's wife, who was a singer and dancer. The act was part of a vaudeville show called *Hippity Hop* that also included other singers, dancers, musicians, and comedians.

Basie and Williams toured with *Hippity Hop* for almost a year, traveling all around the United States. The tour brought Basie to the South for the first time, where he experienced the prejudice and segregation that were a fact of life in that part of the country during those days. Basie and the other African American musicians had to stay in "blacks only" hotels and eat in restaurants that served only African Americans. The experience was harsh, but Basie was having too much fun traveling and performing to let it affect him.

Basie returned to Harlem in 1925, after the *Hippity Hop* tour ended. He fell back into the routine of playing wherever he could. At that time, "parlor socials" or "rent parties" were common in Harlem. Residents held these parties as a way to raise money for their rent. Guests were charged a small admission fee, usually one dollar. The party included homemade food and lots of gambling, and a pianist was usually hired to entertain. Basie played at many of these rent parties, as well as at nightclubs, illegal bars called speakeasies, and small concert halls called cabarets.

The Harlem clubs were the site of a popular form of entertainment called cutting contests. These contests pitted one musician against another. One musician would play a few choruses and then another would step in and create new musical patterns and improvisations on the same tune. The two would go back and forth for hours, with the audience cheering them on. Things could get very heated. Harlem musician Garvin Bushell witnessed many cutting contests during the 1920s. He recalled, "There'd be more controversy among the listeners than the participants. There was betting and people were ready to fight about who'd won."[2] Basie often participated in these contests, along with other pianists. He enjoyed the competition, but he also studied the other pianists closely, looking for ways to improve his own technique.

One of the musicians Basie met at rent parties and cutting contests was Thomas Waller, better known as Fats Waller because of his size. Waller and Basie became great friends, and Basie began to follow Waller around just to watch him play. Like Basie, Waller had once been an accompanist for silent movies, where he learned to improvise in order to match the music to the mood of the film. Waller also taught Basie new techniques on the piano, such as changing chords and repeating some of the notes. Basie later said that Waller had completely changed his style of playing. Waller went on to compose such classics as "Ain't Misbehavin'" and "Honeysuckle Rose" before his untimely death in 1943.

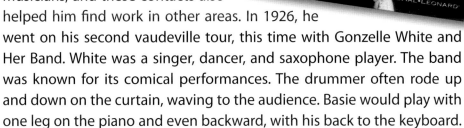

Basie found steady work in Harlem. He got to know many musicians, and these contacts also helped him find work in other areas. In 1926, he went on his second vaudeville tour, this time with Gonzelle White and Her Band. White was a singer, dancer, and saxophone player. The band was known for its comical performances. The drummer often rode up and down on the curtain, waving to the audience. Basie would play with one leg on the piano and even backward, with his back to the keyboard.

Performing with Gonzelle White changed Basie's life and career. One morning, when the band was in Tulsa, Oklahoma, Basie heard music that got him really excited. He rushed out of his hotel room and saw a group of musicians performing from the back of a truck. The group was the Blue Devils, and they were promoting at a dance they'd be playing that evening. Their vocalist, Jimmy Rushing, explained, "The first time he heard the Blue Devils, we were ballyhooing on a big truck. . . . There was a lot of that in those days. Wherever you were working, you had to go out and ballyhoo for the place. Coming back from downtown we struck up a good blues. Basie heard this and . . . ran down and met all the fellows."[3] Basie had never seen a band like this before. They did not use sheet music, yet every musician seemed to know exactly what to play and how to work together.

Basie wasted no time in meeting the band and showing off his piano skills. Rushing really liked Basie's style. "We used to say, 'That guy's crazy' because he played so good," Rushing recalled.[4] Basie had to move on to the next city with his own act, but he and the Blue Devils promised to stay in touch.

The next stop on the vaudeville tour was Kansas City, Missouri. Unfortunately, it was also the last. The band had no more appearances scheduled, and they hadn't saved any money to get back to New York. Basie was stranded in Kansas City.

However, being stuck in Kansas City in 1927 was not a bad thing for a jazz musician. Basie quickly discovered that Kansas City had a thriving music scene. There were hundreds of bars and nightclubs. Music was always playing, and there was plenty of work for everyone. Pianist Mary Lou Williams said, "I found Kansas City to be a heavenly city—music everywhere in the Negro section of town, and fifty or more cabarets rocking on Twelfth and Eighteenth Streets."[5]

Unfortunately, Basie could not take advantage of the Kansas City music scene right away. He became very sick with a serious disease called spinal meningitis and spent four months in the hospital. He recovered, but he had huge medical bills to pay. Desperate to find work, he accepted a job as an organist accompanying movies at a local theater. Basie was given sheet music to play, but he could not always read the notes. Instead, he improvised, using the techniques his friend Fats Waller had taught him back in New York.

By 1928, Basie was a confident and experienced musician. He could play just about any style of jazz and was just as comfortable playing for a rowdy crowd in a bar as he was for dancers in a club. He recalled his meeting with the Blue Devils and how much he admired them. He wrote to the band's leader, Walter Page, asking if they could get together. Page remembered the young piano player and wrote back, inviting Basie to join the band. Basie wasted no time. He packed his bags and headed back out on the road with his first big band.

The Vaudeville Circuit

Between the 1880s and the 1930s, vaudeville was the most popular form of entertainment in the United States and Canada. Vaudeville was a type of stage entertainment that was like a huge variety show. Acts included musicians, singers, dancers, comedians, acrobats, animal acts, magicians, jugglers, actors, and more.

Vaudeville had its beginnings in variety shows that were performed in cities and frontier settlements during the 1850s and 1860s. These shows were meant mostly for men and were not suitable for family entertainment. Then, in 1881, a singer named Tony Pastor created the first variety show for families. Theater managers realized that this type of show would bring more people to the theater and sell more tickets. Vaudeville was born.

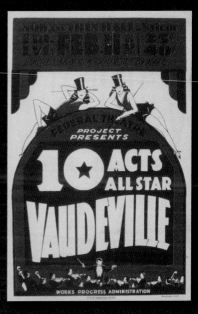

Most vaudeville groups traveled on a circuit, or tour, sometimes performing in a different theater or concert hall every night. Circuits were often tailored to specific ethnic groups. The Theater Owners Booking Association, or TOBA, was a major vaudeville circuit for African American performers, including Count Basie. Other circuits existed for Italian entertainers and Jewish entertainers. Vaudeville shows introduced many people to other cultures and helped break down barriers between different ethnic groups.

By the 1930s, movie theaters found it cheaper to show films than to hire the large number of performers that made up a vaudeville act. Vaudeville's days were over, but many famous actors, musicians, and other performers got their start in the industry.

Chapter 4

The Count Basie Orchestra

Basie joined up with the Blue Devils in Oklahoma City and spent the next year traveling with them through Texas, Kansas, and parts of the Midwest. Being in a big band was a new experience for him. The Blue Devils were known as a territory band. These bands worked in a specific part of the country and competed against other bands that passed through their territory. These competitions were like bigger versions of the cutting contests Basie had experienced in Harlem. Thousands of people would gather for the shows and watch the bands take turns playing and trying to outdo each other in both skill and energy. The band that got the biggest reaction from the audience was the winner.

Being part of the Blue Devils also showed Basie how a large group of musicians could work together. Each member had a say in the group's plans, and all expenses and earnings were equally divided. Basie liked how the band functioned as a community, and he liked that each member had a say, just as each member's instrument was an important part of the band's sound. The pianist made many good friends in the Blue Devils and later said that the group "was just like a beautiful family."[1]

Basie loved his time with the Blue Devils, but he missed the Kansas City music scene. In 1929, he left the Blue Devils to return to Kansas City. Once there, he began playing in clubs. He often took part in jam sessions with other musicians. Sometimes these sessions went on all night, with musicians improvising for hours. One musician recalled a time when he left a jam session at ten o'clock at night, went home to rest, and then went back at one in the morning, only to find that the other musicians were still playing the same song. Trumpeter Buck Clayton recalled a night when one trumpet player after another got up to play. "As the evening wore on, more and more trumpet players came in to blow. To me, it seemed as if they were coming from all directions. Soon the room was just full of trumpet players. They were coming from under the rug, out of the woodwork, behind doors, everywhere. I never saw so many trumpet players in my life."[2]

Buck Clayton

Whenever he wasn't playing, Basie was going to clubs to listen to other bands. Soon after he returned to Kansas City, he went to hear a band called the Bennie Moten Orchestra. Basie was impressed by the band's smooth sound, which was unlike the rowdier music of the Blue Devils. He got to know members of the band and made some suggestions on how their songs could be arranged. He impressed Moten with his talent and musical knowledge. It wasn't long before Moten invited Basie to join the band as a pianist and also help with its musical direction. Basie accepted and remained with the orchestra for the next six years.

Playing with Moten was an important learning experience for Basie, because Moten was both the band's piano player and its leader. The two men often performed together. Sometimes

The Bennie Moten Orchestra performs in the typical style of big band orchestras. Count Basie is seated at the piano at left, while Moten stands second from the right.

they played at the same piano and other times they played on two different pianos placed back to back. "That was such a wonderful learning experience for me because it put me so close to Bennie himself and the way he handled the band from the piano. It was one of the most important experiences a future bandleader could have had," Basie later explained.[3]

Basie toured all over the Midwest, Southwest, and East Coast with the Bennie Moten Orchestra. While in Chicago during 1929, Basie made his first record, which was called "Rumba Negro." He would go on to record many songs with the orchestra over the next few years.

By 1933, the United States was in the middle of the Great Depression, and times were hard for traveling bands. Many times, the group would run out of money and have to stay in a town until Moten managed to book another performance. Musicians joined the group but would leave quickly if they found a better-paying job. Finally, band members had enough. In 1933, during a stop at the Cherry Blossom Theater in Kansas City, band members voted to kick Moten out of the band. To Basie's surprise, they elected him the new bandleader. Basie felt bad because he was a good friend of Moten's, but Moten encouraged him to take the opportunity, since it was what the other members wanted. That night, the group performed under a new name: Count Basie and His Cherry Blossom Orchestra. It was the first time Basie was listed as the head of his own band.

However, Basie had no better luck making money leading the band than Moten had. By early 1935, Basie and several other musicians joined up with Moten again. Moten booked an important gig for them at the Rainbow Gardens in Denver, Colorado. The band traveled west without Moten. He stayed behind in Kansas City to have his tonsils removed and planned to join the band later on. However, something went terribly wrong during the operation, and Moten bled to death. No one in the orchestra had the heart to go on after Moten's sudden death, and the band broke up a few weeks later.

Basie went back to Kansas City and accepted a job as the leader of the house band at the Reno Club. He assembled a top-notch band, including several of his friends from the Blue Devils, such as Jimmy Rushing and Walter Page. Now known as Count Basie and His Barons of Rhythm, this was the band that caught John Hammond's attention and helped bring Basie to national attention.

Hammond wanted to bring Basie and his band to Chicago and New York City. In the fall of 1936, the band left Kansas City. At Hammond's suggestion, Basie had added a trombone section and another tenor saxophone, bringing the band's size up to fifteen members, including Basie. The band was now known simply as Count Basie and His Orchestra. Basie was eager to use Hammond's ideas and follow him out of Kansas City. "I was always willing to say, 'Let's see what happens,' when something came up that looked like it might help me get a little closer to where I wanted to be," he once said.[4]

Singer Jimmy Rushing gestures to the audience while Count Basie plays the piano at a crowded show. Basie and Rushing first met when Basie introduced himself to the band the Blue Devils. They went on to perform and record together many times.

It took some time for the new lineup to figure out how to work together. On Christmas Eve in 1936, the band played a shaky show at the famed Roseland Ballroom in New York City. Critic George Simon wrote, "If you don't believe the band is out of tune, just listen to the reed section. If you don't believe the reed section is out of tune, just listen to the brass section. And if you don't believe that, just listen to the band!"[5]

Fortunately, the more they played together, the better the band sounded. The band members were also fiercely loyal to Basie and refused to leave him. They had so much fun playing together that they were willing to endure the hard times.

REVEILLE with BEVERLY
A COLUMBIA PICTURE

COLUMBIA PICTURES

COUNT BASIE AND HIS UNDISPUTED KINGS OF JIVE!

It was common for big bands to appear in movies. This poster advertises Count Basie's performance in *Reveille with Beverly* in 1943. The movie also featured other popular artists, including Duke Ellington, Frank Sinatra, The Mills Brothers, and Bob Crosby.

In 1937, Count Basie and His Orchestra debuted at Harlem's legendary Apollo Theater. The Apollo was one of the most important places a jazz band could play, and it was known for its highly critical audience. If the audience at the Apollo didn't like you, they would let you know. But if they did like you, your career would fly high.

Basie was understandably nervous before the show at the Apollo. His mood was not helped by a stagehand who stood backstage mocking and teasing Basie while the bandleader waited in the wings to go on. However, the band sounded great and the crowd roared its approval. The concert was one of the band's most important engagements. It showed that Basie had passed the test and was accepted by the toughest jazz fans in the world.

When Did Basie Become the Count?

There are different stories about how and when Basie got his nickname. The most common states that a radio announcer at the Reno Club commented that "Bill Basie" was too ordinary and that there were other bandleaders with "royal" names, such as Earl Hines, King Oliver, and Duke Ellington. He suggested that Basie call himself "Count Basie," and Basie agreed without thinking much of it.

However, Basie himself said that this story wasn't true. He points out that the first time he was called "Count" was the billing for Count Basie and His Cherry Blossom Orchestra in 1933, several years before his appearance at the Reno. In his autobiography, Basie said that he called himself "Count" even before he played at the Cherry Blossom. Basie said that Bennie Moten actually gave him the nickname. Sometimes Moten would come looking for Basie, and if the piano player couldn't be found, Moten would say, "Where is that no 'count rascal?" Basie also said that he printed some business cards that said, "Beware. The Count Is Here" when he arrived in Kansas City in 1927. The true origin of Basie's nickname may never be known, but it certainly became well known to music fans around the world.

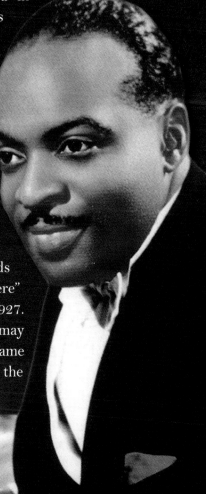

The Band Lives On

Count Basie and his band were at the top of their game in the late 1930s. In 1937, the band recorded a song called "One O'Clock Jump." This song was originally written while the band was based in Kansas City. It became a huge hit and a favorite of dancers everywhere. Many other bands recorded the song, including the Benny Goodman Orchestra. By 1940, "One O'Clock Jump" had been recorded at least a dozen times, and it would go on to become one of the classics of the big band era.

In 1938, Basie's band played two memorable concerts in one night. On January 16, 1938, Basie and four of his musicians joined Benny Goodman and his band as special guests for a historic concert at New York City's Carnegie Hall. It was the first time jazz had been presented at the concert hall, and Basie thrilled the audience with his performance.

After the Carnegie Hall concert was over, Basie and his band headed uptown to the Savoy Ballroom, where they performed in a showdown against the popular Chick Webb Orchestra. The two bands battled it out in front of thousands of fans, including such notables as Duke Ellington, Lionel Hampton, and Benny Goodman. When the battle was finally over, the audience's reaction indicated that Webb's orchestra was the winner. However, most of the critics and musicians who were there proclaimed that Basie's band had triumphed. Either way, it was an amazing and unforgettable night for jazz fans.

Count Basie poses with "the King of Swing," Benny Goodman, and vocalist Ethel Waters during a performance for soldiers during World War II. Popular artists often entertained the troops at special nightclubs and theater performances during the war.

For the next few years, Basie and his band were the kings of jazz and swing music. The Count Basie Orchestra took a fresh approach to this style of music. Unlike other bands, the beat was steady and smooth, but not heavy. The bass created a steady pulse, while the guitar made waves that moved the beat along. Writer Wilder Hobson described the orchestra's sound like this: "The band plays with apparent effortlessness, fourteen men attacking as freely and spiritedly as five might do, always giving a sense of ample reserve power."[1]

Perhaps the most distinctive feature of the Basie sound was Basie's piano playing. Unlike other jazz pianists, Basie did not show off or allow the piano to dominate the orchestra's sound. Instead, he had a stripped-down style with fewer notes. His motto was to play less but make every note count. One of his band members described Basie's spare style by saying, "Count don't play nothing, but it sure sounds good."[2] Basie's style actually changed the role of the piano in jazz music. Instead of playing melody, as most pianists did, Basie used the piano as a rhythm instrument, adding to and smoothing out the beats.

Basie's fresh sound also came from his use of the blues. Basie was the first to take the riffs and blues patterns popular in Kansas City music and fuse them with the big band sound to create a new kind of jazz. These arrangements were never written down. Instead, they were known as head arrangements because the musicians memorized them and kept them in their heads. It was not uncommon for Basie and his band to perform all evening with only four or five sheets of music for the whole concert.

Basie's unique sound made him one of the country's most popular and best-known African American bandleaders. Only Duke Ellington was his equal. During the 1940s, the Count Basie Orchestra was appearing regularly in New York's hottest concert halls and theaters. The band also toured the country several times, performing almost every night.

The early 1940s brought both sorrow and happiness to Basie in his personal life. His beloved mother died in 1941. Basie missed her, but he was thrilled that she had lived long enough to see his success. Basie suffered another loss when his good friend, Fats Waller, died suddenly of pneumonia in 1943. On a happier note, Basie married a vaudeville dancer named Catherine Morgan in 1942. The two had known each other for many years. Catherine gave birth to their daughter, Diane, in

Although he was on the road a lot, Count Basie was devoted to his wife and children. Here, he and his wife and daughter, Diane, enjoy listening to a tape of a Basie recording.

1944. The Basies went on to adopt two sons and a daughter over the next few years.

Although Basie remained extremely popular through the first half of the 1940s, musical tastes began to change in the latter part of that decade. Big band music was no longer as popular and was being replaced by pop singers. By 1950, Basie could no longer afford to keep his band together. The Count Basie Orchestra disbanded that year, but Basie's career was far from over.

Soon after his big band split, Basie put together a smaller band of only six musicians. The group played steadily, but Basie was not satisfied. He missed the sound of a big band, as well as the interplay between performers. Basie joked that he had to work too hard without other band members performing. Finally, he realized that he would not be happy unless he was leading a big band. In 1952, the new Count Basie Orchestra debuted at New York City's Birdland Jazz Club. The concert went well, and Basie was able to successfully tour the country with his new big band.

In May 1955, vocalist Joe Williams recorded "Every Day I Have the Blues" with the Count Basie Orchestra. The song became a big hit and introduced Basie to younger fans. It became one of the orchestra's most popular songs.

Basie continued to perform and tour over the next thirty years. In the 1960s, he performed at the inaugurations of President John F. Kennedy and President Lyndon B. Johnson. Also during the 1960s, he worked with an up-and-coming arranger named Quincy Jones, scoring many tops hits. Basie also recorded with some of America's most popular singers, including Ella Fitzgerald, Tony Bennett, Frank Sinatra, and Sammy Davis Jr. During the 1970s, Basie toured around the world. A heart attack in 1976 temporarily slowed him down, but he was back on tour six months later. One of his band members joked that Basie was too used to being on the road to quit.

However, Basie's declining health eventually forced him to slow down. His wife died in 1983. Basie performed a few concerts during the following year and also worked on his autobiography, *Good Morning*

Count Basie continued to perform almost until his death. Here he leads his band on *Big Bands from the Dorchester*, which was broadcast in 1974. This British television series featured many popular big bands.

Blues. Then, on April 26, 1984, Count Basie died of cancer. His band members, family, and friends gathered in a huge crowd to say goodbye at his funeral.

Basie was gone, but the Count Basie Orchestra lives on. The orchestra still tours, performing and delighting listeners around the world. Basie once said, "All I wanted [was] to be big, to be in show business and to travel, and that's what I've been doing all my life."[3] It was a life that would bring great pleasure to himself and everyone around him—and change the face of jazz music forever.

Kansas City
Jazz

Kansas City jazz had a distinct sound that was different from jazz in other parts of the country. Kansas City jazz featured two important elements, riffs and blues. Riffs are short musical phrases that are played over and over by the instruments in a band. One musician might come up with a riff during a jam session, and then other members of the band would join in and play it on their instruments. Riffs provided great music for dancing because they were repeated over and over and created a wave of sound that kept the music moving.

Kansas City jazz also included the blues. The blues is a distinct type of African American music that originated after the Civil War. The blues combined work songs sung by slaves with church songs called spirituals. The combination created repetitive, often sad music that conveyed great pain and longing. Blues music usually repeats four measures of notes three times, with musicians improvising melodies and adding chords. Blues vocalists usually sang about everyday concerns, such as romances gone bad, loneliness, hard work, and misfortune. However, the blues form could be adapted to create happy, upbeat music as well. It was a simple yet ever-changing style that created a unique type of music when combined with riffs and the fast-paced rhythms of jazz.

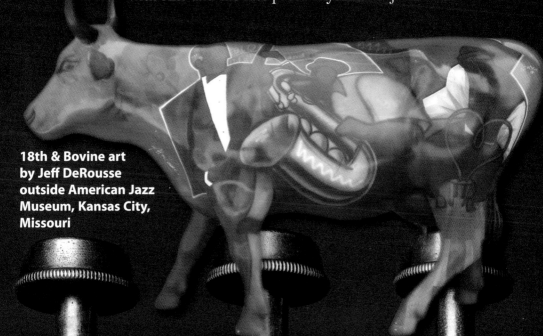

18th & Bovine art by Jeff DeRousse outside American Jazz Museum, Kansas City, Missouri

1904 William "Bill" Basie is born in Red Bank, New Jersey, on August 21.

1924 He moves to New York City; tours the U.S. with the *Hippity Hop* vaudeville show.

1926 He tours with the vaudeville act Gonzelle White and Her Band; meets the Blue Devils band for the first time.

1927 With Gonzelle White, he travels to Kansas City, Missouri, where he is stranded with no money.

1928 He joins the Blue Devils.

1929 He joins the Bennie Moten Orchestra and tours with them; his first recording, "Rumba Negro," is made with them.

1933 He takes over as the leader of the Bennie Moten Orchestra and changes its name to Count Basie and His Cherry Blossom Orchestra.

1935 Basie becomes the bandleader at Kansas City's Reno Club; he meets John Hammond.

1936 Basie forms Count Basie and His Orchestra and moves to New York City to record and perform.

1937 The orchestra debuts at the famous Apollo Theater in Harlem; it records "One O'Clock Jump."

1938 Basie and his orchestra appear at Benny Goodman's legendary Carnegie Hall concert on January 16; later that night, he is in a showdown against the Chick Webb Orchestra at the Savoy Ballroom.

1942 Basie marries Catherine Morgan.

1950 The Count Basie Orchestra disbands.

1952 A new Count Basie Orchestra debuts.

1955 Basie records the hit song "Every Day I Have the Blues" with vocalist Big Joe Williams.

1961 He performs at President John F. Kennedy's inauguration.

1965 He performs at President Lyndon B. Johnson's inauguration.

1976 He suffers a heart attack and recovers.

1983 Catherine Morgan Basie dies.

1984 Count Basie dies of cancer on April 26; the Monmouth Arts Center in Red Bank, New Jersey, is renamed the Count Basie Theatre.

1985 *Good Morning Blues,* his autobiography as told to Albert Murray, is published.

Discography

Count Basie played on hundreds of albums, and it is impossible to list them all here. This discography includes the most popular and important albums of his career.

1937 Basie's Best
1941 Café Society Uptown
1942 Blues by Basie
1944 Count Basie and His Orchestra
1951 One O'Clock Jump
1952 Basie Rides Again!
1954 New Year at Birdland
      Class of '54
1955 Count Basie Swings/Joe Williams Sings
      April in Paris
1957 Count Basie at Newport
      Atomic Basie
1958 Sing Along with Basie
      Basie/Bennett
1959 Every Day I Have the Blues

1960 Not Now, I'll Tell You When
      Count Basie/Sarah Vaughan
1961 The Legend
      First Time! The Count Meets
         the Duke
1962 Back with Basie
      Sinatra-Basie
1964 It Might As Well Be Swing
1969 Jazz Fest Masters: Count Basie
1975 Fun Time at Montreux
1976 I Told You So
1980 Kansas City Shout
1983 Me and You
      88 Basie Street

Chapter 1. The Man at the Piano

1. Count Basie, *Good Morning Blues* (New York: Random House, 1985), p. 165.
2. Ibid., p. 166.
3. Rock and Roll Hall of Fame Museum: "John Hammond Biography," retrieved August 8, 2011, http://rockhall.com/inductees/john-hammond/bio/

Chapter 2. The Boy from Red Bank

1. Count Basie, *Good Morning Blues* (New York: Random House, 1985), pp. 26–27.
2. Ibid., p. 45.

Chapter 3. From New York to Kansas City

1. Count Basie, *Good Morning Blues* (New York: Random House, 1985), p. 53.
2. Lawrence W. Levine, *Black Culture and Black Consciousness* (New York: Oxford University Press, 1978), p. 234.
3. Stanley Dance, *The World of Count Basie* (New York: Da Capo Press, 1980), p. 20.
4. Ibid.
5. "In Her Own Words . . . Mary Lou Williams Interview," *Melody Maker,* April–June 1954, retrieved August 4, 2011, http://www.ratical.org/MaryLouWilliams/MMiview1954.html

Chapter 4. The Count Basie Orchestra

1. Count Basie, *Good Morning Blues* (New York: Random House, 1985), p. 18.
2. Buck Clayton and Nancy Miller Elliott, *Buck Clayton's Jazz World* (New York: Continuum International Publishing Group, 1995), p. 90.
3. Basie, p. 122.
4. Ibid., p. 385.
5. Stanley Dance, *The World of Count Basie* (New York: Da Capo Press, 1980), p. 4.

Chapter 5. The Band Lives On

1. Quoted in "Count Basie," *Current Biography,* retrieved August 4, 2011, http://cms.westport.k12.ct.us/cmslmc/music/jazzbios/basie.htm

2. Barry Ulanov, *A History of Jazz in America* (New York: The Viking Press, 1955), p. 190.

3. "Count Basie Quotes." ThinkExist.com, retrieved July 29, 2011, http://thinkexist.com/quotes/count_basie/

BOOKS

While at the time of this printing there were no other books about Count Basie available for children, you might enjoy these other jazz musician books from Mitchell Lane Publishers:

Boone, Mary. *Dizzy Gillespie.* Hockessin, DE: Mitchell Lane Publishers, 2013.

Orr, Tamra. *Louis Armstrong.* Hockessin, DE: Mitchell Lane Publishers, 2013.

Rice, Earle, Jr. *Billie Holiday.* Hockessin, DE: Mitchell Lane Publishers, 2013.

Roberts, Russell. *Scott Joplin.* Hockessin, DE: Mitchell Lane Publishers, 2013.

Tracy, Kathleen. *Bessie Smith.* Hockessin, DE: Mitchell Lane Publishers, 2013.

WORKS CONSULTED

Basie, Count. *Good Morning Blues.* New York: Random House, 1985.

Clayton, Buck, and Nancy Miller Elliott. *Buck Clayton's Jazz World.* New York: Continuum International Publishing Group, 1995.

"Count Basie Quotes." ThinkExist.com http://thinkexist.com/quotes/count_basie/

Dance, Stanley. *The World of Count Basie.* New York: Da Capo Press, 1980.

HyperMusic: "A History of Jazz." http://www.hypermusic.ca/jazz/mainmenu.html

"In Her Own Words . . . Mary Lou Williams Interview." *Melody Maker,* April–June 1954. http://www.ratical.org/MaryLouWilliams/MMiview1954.html

Jazz, a Film by Ken Burns. Hollywood: Paramount Home Video and PBS Home Video, 2004.

Levine, Lawrence W. *Black Culture and Black Consciousness.* New York: Oxford University Press, 1978.

PBS—American Masters: "Vaudeville." http://www.pbs.org/wnet/americanmasters/episodes/vaudeville/about-vaudeville/721/

Red Hot Jazz: "Thomas 'Fats' Waller." http://www.redhotjazz.com/
fats.html

Rock and Roll Hall of Fame Museum: "John Hammond Biography."
http://rockhall.com/inductees/john-hammond/bio/

SwingMusic.net: "Big Band Battle of Bands Count Basie vs. Chick Webb."
http://www.swingmusic.net/Swing_Music_Chick_Webb_Cuts_
Count_Basie.html

SwingMusic.net Biography: "Count Basie." http://www.swingmusic.net/
Count_Basie.html

Ulanov, Barry. *A History of Jazz in America.* New York: The Viking Press,
1955.

ON THE INTERNET

"Count Basie." *Current Biography,* 1942, online at
http://cms.westport.k12.ct.us/cmslmc/music/jazzbios/basie.htm

Count Basie Theatre
http://www.countbasietheatre.org/

"Hey, Kids, Meet Count Basie." Making Music Fun.
http://www.makingmusicfun.net/htm/f_mmf_music_library/
hey-kids-its-count-basie.htm

PBS JAZZ—Selected Artist Biography. "Jazz Greats: Benny Goodman."
http://www.pbs.org/jazz/biography/artist_id_goodman_benny.htm

PBS JAZZ—Selected Artist Biography. "Jazz Greats: Count Basie."
http://www.pbs.org/jazz/biography/artist_id_basie_count.htm

accompanist (uh-KUM-puh-nist)—Someone who accompanies, or plays an instrument with, a singer.

arrangement (uh-RANJ-munt)—An adaptation of a musical composition so that it can be played by an orchestra.

brass (BRASS)—An instrument made of brass that has a metal mouthpiece, such as a trumpet, trombone, or tuba.

cabaret (KAB-uh-ray)—A nightclub that puts on shows including music and dancing.

chord (KORD)—A combination of two or more notes played together.

improvisation (im-prah-vih-ZAY-shun)—The making up of music as it is performed.

jam session (JAM SEH-shun)—An informal performance by a group of musicians that often includes improvisation.

pianist (PEE-uh-nist)—A person who plays the piano.

reed (REED)—A woodwind instrument that has at least one reed (a thin piece of wood) in the mouthpiece, such as a saxophone, clarinet, or bassoon.

riff (RIF)—A short musical passage played over and over.

vaudeville (VAWD-vil)—Stage entertainment that includes various acts, such as singers, dancers, comedians, animal tricks, and acrobats.

vocalist (VOH-kuh-list)—A singer.

Index

About the Author

Joanne Mattern is the author of more than 200 nonfiction books for young readers. Her books for Mitchell Lane include biographies of such notables as Michelle Obama, Benny Goodman, Blake Lively, Selena, LeBron James, and Peyton Manning. Mattern grew up listening to big band, jazz, and popular music and hearing stories of how her father saw most of the big band artists perform, including his favorite, Count Basie. She also studied piano and voice for many years. Mattern lives in New York State with her husband, four children, and an assortment of pets.